# CONTENTS

# INTRODUCTION

Life is full of challenges and obstacles that can make it difficult to achieve our goals and reach our full potential. It's easy to get discouraged when things don't go as planned or when setbacks and failures occur. However, the truth is that these challenges are opportunities to grow, to learn, and to become stronger.

In this book, we will explore the concept of resilience and how it can help us overcome adversity and achieve our dreams. We will dive into the topics of networking, work-life balance, failure, technology, leadership, change, negotiation, education, time management, mindset, personal branding, ethics, and problem-solving. Through personal anecdotes, research, and practical strategies, we will show you how to build resilience, overcome obstacles, and achieve success in both your personal and professional life.

Our hope is that this book will inspire you to push beyond your limits, to see challenges as opportunities, and to reach your full potential. Let's dive in!

# DEVELOPING A SUCCESSFUL CAREER

Your career is a major aspect of your life, and it can bring you not only financial stability but also personal fulfillment. However, building a successful career requires more than just luck or natural talent. It takes a deliberate and strategic approach to developing the skills, experience, and reputation that can help you stand out in your industry and achieve your goals.

In this chapter, we'll explore some key principles and strategies for building a successful career, including:

Identifying your strengths and interests: Understanding your strengths, interests, and values can help you choose a career path that aligns with your passions and talents. Take the time to reflect on what motivates and excites you, and seek out opportunities that allow you to use your unique skills and abilities.

Building a strong foundation: Developing a strong foundation of knowledge, skills, and experience is essential for building a successful career. This may involve pursuing formal education, gaining practical experience through internships or entry-level jobs, and building a network of mentors and peers who can offer guidance and support.

Focusing on continuous learning and development: The world is constantly changing, and staying up-to-date on the latest trends and technologies in your industry is crucial for staying competitive. Make a commitment to continuous learning and development, whether through formal education, professional development programs, or self-directed learning.

Developing a strong work ethic: Success in any career requires hard work, dedication, and a commitment to excellence. Cultivate a strong work ethic by setting high standards for yourself, focusing on results, and consistently delivering high-quality work.

Building a personal brand: Your reputation and personal brand are key factors in building a successful career. Develop a strong online presence, cultivate a network of professional contacts, and focus on delivering value to your clients or customers.

By following these principles and strategies, you can build a successful career that not only meets your financial needs but also provides personal fulfillment and a sense of purpose.

# IDENTIFYING YOUR STRENGTHS AND INTERESTS

Identifying your strengths and interests is a crucial first step in developing a successful career. When you understand what you are good at and what you enjoy doing, you can more easily choose a career path that aligns with your passions and talents.

Take the time to reflect on what motivates and excites you. Consider your hobbies, extracurricular activities, and any tasks you naturally gravitate towards. What are the common threads that run through these activities? Perhaps you enjoy problem-solving, helping others, or being creative. Think about what energizes you and makes you feel fulfilled.

Another way to identify your strengths is to ask others for feedback. Your friends, family, and colleagues may have insights about your abilities that you haven't considered. They may see talents in you that you take for granted or don't realize you possess.

Once you have a good understanding of your strengths and interests, you can start exploring career paths that align with them. Research various industries and job roles to find opportunities that match your skills and passions. Seek out networking events and informational interviews to learn more about the day-to-day responsibilities of various roles and industries.

Ultimately, identifying your strengths and interests will help you choose a career path that is fulfilling and allows you to reach your full potential. When you are passionate about your work, it becomes easier to put in the effort required to achieve your goals and succeed in your career.

# BUILDING A STRONG FOUNDATION

Building a strong foundation: Developing a strong foundation of knowledge, skills, and experience is essential for building a successful career. While formal education can be helpful, it's not always necessary. Many successful people have foregone university and instead pursued practical experience through internships, entry-level jobs, and self-learning.

For instance, Steve Jobs, co-founder of Apple, dropped out of college after just six months to pursue his passion for technology. He went on to build one of the most successful companies in the world. Similarly, Mark Zuckerberg, founder of Facebook, left Harvard after just two years to focus on building his social media platform.

The key is to pursue opportunities that allow you to gain practical experience and build a network of mentors and peers who can offer guidance and support. This may involve taking on internships or entry-level jobs in your desired field, attending industry events and conferences, and seeking out mentorship from experienced professionals.

By building a strong foundation of knowledge, skills, and experience, you can position yourself for success and open up a world of possibilities for your career.

# CONTINUOUSLY LEARNING AND GROWING

Continuously Learning and Growing: To succeed in your career, it's essential to stay updated on the latest trends and advancements in your industry. This means making a commitment to continuous learning and growth. Whether you choose to pursue formal education, attend professional development programs or conferences, or engage in self-directed learning, the key is to be open to new ideas and approaches. By continuously expanding your knowledge and skills, you can stay ahead of the curve and remain competitive in the job market. Moreover, you can discover new opportunities and interests that can lead to exciting career prospects. Remember, learning is a lifelong process, and a commitment to growth can be a key ingredient in your recipe for success.

## A Strong Work Ethic

A strong work ethic is a fundamental building block of a successful career. Regardless of the industry or profession, hard work, dedication, and a commitment to excellence are key factors that set top performers apart from the rest. To develop a strong work ethic, it is essential to set high standards for yourself, prioritize your work, and focus on results. One of the most effective ways to cultivate a strong work ethic is by setting clear goals and objectives. This can help you stay focused and motivated, and ensure that you are consistently working towards achieving your desired outcomes. Be specific in your goal setting, and make sure that each goal is measurable and achievable.

Another important aspect of building a strong work ethic is learning to prioritize your work effectively. This means identifying the most important tasks and projects and focusing your time and energy on those that will have the greatest impact. This can involve making tough decisions about which tasks to tackle first, and learning to manage your time effectively to ensure that you are making progress towards your goals.

Finally, to develop a strong work ethic, it is essential to consistently deliver high-quality work. This means taking pride in your work, paying attention to detail, and striving for excellence in everything you do. Whether you are working on a small project or a major initiative, approach each task with a sense of purpose and a commitment to delivering the best possible results.

By focusing on developing a strong work ethic, you can set yourself up for success in any career. By prioritizing your work, setting clear goals, and consistently delivering high-quality results, you can demonstrate your value to your employer, build a reputation as a top performer, and achieve your career goals.

# BUILDING A PERSONAL BRAND

In today's digital age, building a personal brand is crucial for career success. Your personal brand represents how you are perceived by others in your industry, and can be the deciding factor in whether or not you are offered new opportunities or promotions. Here are some tips for building a strong personal brand:

Develop a strong online presence: Your online presence can have a significant impact on your personal brand. Create a professional website or blog that showcases your skills and expertise, and use social media to connect with others in your industry and share your knowledge and insights.

Cultivate a network of professional contacts: Building relationships with others in your industry is essential for building a strong personal brand. Attend industry events, join professional organizations, and connect with others on LinkedIn to expand your network and learn from others.

Focus on delivering value: Your personal brand should be built around the value you bring to your clients or customers. Focus on delivering high-quality work, providing excellent customer service, and going above and beyond to meet the needs of your clients or customers.

Be authentic: Your personal brand should be a reflection of who you truly are. Be true to yourself, and focus on developing a personal brand that represents your values, interests, and expertise.

By focusing on building a strong personal brand, you can establish yourself as a thought leader in your industry and open up new opportunities for career growth and advancement.

# ACHIEVING WORK-LIFE BALANCE:

In today's fast-paced world, achieving a healthy work-life balance can be a challenge. Juggling work responsibilities, personal commitments, and family obligations can often leave individuals feeling stressed and overwhelmed. However, it's crucial to find the right balance in order to live a fulfilling life and maintain long-term success in your career. In this chapter, we will explore the importance of work-life balance and provide practical strategies for achieving it.

I. The Importance of Work-Life Balance

- The impact of work-life balance on personal health and well-being
- The impact of work-life balance on job satisfaction and productivity
- The challenges of achieving work-life balance in today's society

II. Building Resilience: How to Bounce Back from Setbacks and Keep Moving Forward

- The importance of resilience in achieving work-life balance
- Strategies for building resilience in the face of setbacks and challenges
- Tips for maintaining a positive outlook and avoiding burnout

III. Navigating Change in Your Career: Strategies for Adapting to

New Opportunities and Challenges

- The role of change in achieving work-life balance
- Strategies for navigating career changes and transitions
- The benefits of embracing change and seeking out new opportunities

In conclusion, achieving work-life balance is essential for living a fulfilling life and achieving long-term success in your career. By building resilience and developing strategies for navigating change, individuals can maintain a healthy work-life balance and find the sweet spot that works for them. It's not always easy, but with the right mindset and approach, anyone can achieve work-life balance and thrive both personally and professionally.

# THE IMPORTANCE OF WORK-LIFE BALANCE

In today's fast-paced society, achieving a balance between work and personal life can be a significant challenge. The demands of work can often spill over into personal time, leaving individuals feeling overwhelmed and stressed. However, maintaining a healthy work-life balance is crucial for both personal and professional success.

One of the most important benefits of work-life balance is its impact on personal health and well-being. When work demands begin to take over personal time, individuals can experience physical and emotional stress, leading to burnout and decreased quality of life. Chronic stress can also lead to long-term health issues such as heart disease, depression, and anxiety.

Moreover, work-life balance also has a significant impact on job satisfaction and productivity. When individuals feel overwhelmed by work demands and unable to prioritize their personal lives, their motivation and job satisfaction can suffer. Conversely, when individuals are able to maintain a healthy balance between work and personal life, they are often more productive, engaged, and satisfied in their work.

However, achieving a work-life balance is not always easy. In today's fast-paced, technology-driven society, work can often feel all-consuming, with constant emails, texts, and calls blurring the lines between work and personal time. Additionally, many individuals face external pressures such as financial obligations, caregiving responsibilities, and social expectations that can make it difficult to prioritize personal time.

Despite these challenges, it is possible to achieve a work-life balance with the right strategies and mindset. In the following sections, we will explore some effective strategies for achieving work-life balance and building resilience in the face of setbacks and challenges. By prioritizing personal health and well-being, setting clear boundaries between work and personal time, and developing a support network of friends and family, individuals can create a fulfilling and sustainable balance between work and personal life.

# BUILDING RESILIENCE: HOW TO BOUNCE BACK FROM SETBACKS AND KEEP MOVING FORWARD

In order to achieve work-life balance and find success in your career and personal life, it's crucial to develop resilience. Resilience is the ability to bounce back from setbacks and challenges and to keep moving forward despite adversity. In this section, we will explore the importance of resilience, and provide strategies for building resilience and maintaining a positive outlook.

A. The importance of resilience in achieving work-life balance
Resilience is a key factor in achieving work-life balance, as it allows you to overcome obstacles and setbacks without getting derailed from your goals. When faced with challenges such as job loss, health issues, or personal difficulties, resilience can help you stay focused and motivated, and keep you on track towards achieving your goals.

B. Strategies for building resilience in the face of setbacks and challenges

There are a number of strategies you can use to build resilience in the face of setbacks and challenges. These include:

Developing a growth mindset: Adopting a growth mindset, where you view challenges as opportunities for learning and growth, can help you build resilience and develop a positive outlook.

Practicing self-care: Taking care of your physical and mental health is essential for building resilience. This may include regular exercise, healthy eating habits, and getting enough rest.

Seeking support: Surrounding yourself with a network of supportive friends and family members can help you build resilience and cope with difficult situations.

Setting realistic goals: Setting realistic goals and breaking them down into achievable steps can help you build resilience by giving you a sense of accomplishment and progress.

C. Tips for maintaining a positive outlook and avoiding burnout

Maintaining a positive outlook and avoiding burnout is key to building and maintaining resilience. Some tips for doing so include:

Focusing on the positive: Cultivating a positive mindset by focusing on your strengths and accomplishments can help you maintain a positive outlook and avoid burnout.

Taking breaks: Taking regular breaks and disconnecting

from work can help you recharge and prevent burnout.

Engaging in enjoyable activities: Pursuing activities that bring you joy and fulfillment can help you maintain a positive outlook and build resilience.

In conclusion, building resilience is essential for achieving work-life balance and finding success in your career and personal life. By developing a growth mindset, practicing self-care, seeking support, setting realistic goals, and maintaining a positive outlook, you can build resilience and bounce back from setbacks and challenges with greater ease and confidence.

# NAVIGATING CHANGE IN YOUR CAREER: STRATEGIES FOR ADAPTING TO NEW OPPORTUNITIES AND CHALLENGES

Change is an inevitable part of life, and the same is true in the world of work. Whether it's a new job opportunity, a shift in company culture, or a major industry disruption, career changes and transitions can be both exciting and challenging. The ability to adapt and navigate change is essential for achieving work-life balance and building a fulfilling career.

In this section, we will explore the role of change in achieving work-life balance and discuss strategies for navigating career changes and transitions. We will also examine the benefits of embracing change and seeking out new opportunities.

Change can often be daunting, especially when it comes to our careers. However, it's important to recognize that change can also be an opportunity for growth and development. When we embrace change and approach it with a positive mindset, we open ourselves up to new possibilities and experiences.

Navigating career changes and transitions requires a mix of preparation, flexibility, and resilience. It's essential to stay informed about industry trends and developments and to develop the skills and knowledge needed to succeed in a rapidly changing job market. Networking and building relationships with mentors and peers can also provide valuable support and guidance during times of change.

Ultimately, the key to successfully navigating change in your career is to remain open-minded and adaptable. Embrace the opportunities that come your way, even if they require stepping outside of your comfort zone. By being willing to take risks and learn from new experiences, you can build a rewarding and fulfilling career that aligns with your values and goals.

# BECOMING AN EFFECTIVE LEADER

Leadership 101: Key Traits of Successful Leaders and How to Develop Them

Effective leadership is a critical component of any successful organization or team. Whether you're managing a team of employees, leading a community group, or even just looking to improve your personal leadership skills, understanding the key traits of successful leaders and how to develop them is essential. In this section, we'll explore some of the most important traits of successful leaders and provide practical strategies for developing your own leadership abilities.

Key traits of successful leaders:

Vision: Successful leaders have a clear vision for the future, and are able to communicate this vision to their team in a way that inspires and motivates them.

Empathy: Good leaders are able to understand and empathize with the perspectives and needs of their team members, and use this understanding to build strong relationships and create a positive, collaborative work environment.

Accountability: Effective leaders take ownership of their decisions and actions, and hold themselves and their team members accountable for achieving their goals and meeting their responsibilities.

Adaptability: The best leaders are able to adapt to changing circumstances and navigate unexpected challenges with flexibility and grace.

Communication: Strong communication skills are essential for effective leadership. Successful leaders are able to communicate their ideas clearly and persuasively, and are skilled at both giving and receiving feedback.

Developing your leadership skills:

Seek out opportunities for growth: Look for opportunities to take on leadership roles, even if they are outside of your comfort zone. Take on new challenges and responsibilities, and don't be afraid to make mistakes or ask for feedback.

Build your network: Connect with other leaders in your industry or community, and seek out mentorship and guidance from those who have more experience.

Focus on self-improvement: Take the time to reflect on your own leadership strengths and weaknesses, and look for opportunities to develop new skills or improve your existing ones.

Practice active listening: Effective leadership requires not only good communication skills, but also the ability to listen actively and attentively to the needs and perspectives of others.

Lead by example: The best leaders set the tone for their team by modeling the behavior they want to see in others. Be honest, accountable, and focused on achieving results, and your team will follow your lead.

Developing effective leadership skills is an ongoing process, but with dedication and practice, anyone can become a successful leader. By focusing on the key traits of successful leaders and taking practical steps to develop your own leadership abilities, you can become a more effective, inspiring, and impactful leader in your career and beyond.

# FINDING YOUR VOICE: HOW TO SPEAK UP AND MAKE AN IMPACT IN YOUR WORKPLACE

To become an effective leader, it's essential to find your voice and learn how to speak up in the workplace. Speaking up can be intimidating, especially if you're new to the job or working in a high-pressure environment. But finding the confidence to express your ideas and opinions is critical to making an impact in your workplace and advancing your career.

Here are some tips for finding your voice and making an impact in your workplace:

Know your strengths: Before you can effectively speak up and make an impact, you need to have a good understanding of your strengths and areas of expertise. Take some time to reflect on your skills and experiences, and think about how you can leverage them to contribute to your team or organization.

Build relationships: Building strong relationships with your colleagues is essential to creating a supportive and collaborative work environment. Take the time to get to know your coworkers, and look for opportunities to collaborate and share ideas.

Speak up: Don't be afraid to speak up and share your ideas and opinions. If you have something to contribute to a discussion or project, make your voice heard. Be respectful and professional, but don't hold back if you have something valuable to contribute.

Listen actively: Effective communication is a two-way street, and listening actively is just as important as speaking up. Make an effort to truly listen to your colleagues' ideas and perspectives, and be open to feedback and constructive criticism.

Be confident: Confidence is key when it comes to finding your voice in the workplace. Believe in yourself and your ideas, and don't be afraid to take risks and step out of your comfort zone.

By following these tips, you can find your voice and make an impact in your workplace. Remember, effective communication is a skill that takes time and practice to develop, but with dedication and perseverance, you can become a confident and influential leader in your organization.

# THE ART OF NEGOTIATION: TIPS FOR GETTING WHAT YOU WANT IN YOUR CAREER AND BEYOND

Negotiation is a crucial skill in both your professional and personal life. It allows you to advocate for yourself and get what you want, whether it's a higher salary, better working conditions, or a successful business deal. But effective negotiation requires more than just making demands and sticking to your guns. It requires careful preparation, effective communication, and a willingness to compromise and find mutually beneficial solutions.

Key Traits of Successful Negotiators

Successful negotiators share several key traits that allow them to navigate difficult conversations and come out on top. These traits include:

Preparation: Successful negotiators prepare thoroughly before entering into negotiations. They research the other party, gather information on their needs and interests, and identify their own goals and priorities.

Flexibility: Effective negotiators are flexible and willing to adjust their approach based on the situation. They listen carefully to the other party and look for creative solutions that meet both parties' needs.

Communication: Successful negotiators are skilled communicators who can clearly articulate their position, actively listen to the other party, and maintain a constructive dialogue throughout the negotiation process.

Patience: Negotiations can be long and complex, and successful negotiators are patient and persistent in pursuing their goals. They understand that reaching a mutually beneficial agreement often requires time and effort.

Tips for Effective Negotiation

If you want to become a successful negotiator, there are several tips you can follow:

Prepare thoroughly: Before entering into negotiations, do your research, identify your goals and priorities, and anticipate the other party's needs and interests.

Listen actively: Effective negotiation requires active listening. Pay attention to the other party's needs and interests, and look for opportunities to find common ground and build rapport.

Communicate clearly: Clearly articulate your position and be open to constructive feedback. Keep the dialogue constructive and avoid making personal attacks or getting defensive.

Look for creative solutions: Effective negotiation often requires finding creative solutions that meet both parties' needs. Be open to compromise and explore options that benefit both parties.

Be patient and persistent: Negotiations can be long and complex, and success often requires patience and persistence. Don't give up too quickly, and be willing to put in the time and effort to reach a mutually beneficial agreement.

Effective negotiation is a key skill for anyone looking to advance their career or achieve their goals. By developing the key traits of successful negotiators and following these tips for effective negotiation, you can become a more confident and effective negotiator, and achieve the outcomes you desire.

# CONTINUING EDUCATION AND SELF-IMPROVEMENT

# THE BENEFITS OF CONTINUING EDUCATION: HOW TO KEEP LEARNING AND GROWING IN YOUR CAREER

In today's fast-paced and constantly changing world, it's essential to keep learning and growing in order to stay competitive in your career. Whether you're seeking to advance in your current job, transition to a new career, or simply improve your skills and knowledge, continuing education and self-improvement are key.

In this section, we'll explore the benefits of continuing education, as well as strategies for mastering time management and boosting productivity to help you achieve your goals.

Continuing education can take many forms, from pursuing a graduate degree to attending conferences, workshops, or webinars. The benefits of continuing education are numerous, including:

Enhanced job performance: Continuing education can help you stay up-to-date on the latest trends and technologies in your industry, and provide you with the skills and knowledge needed to perform your job at a high level.

Career advancement: Earning additional credentials or certifications can make you a more competitive candidate for promotions or new job opportunities.

Personal growth: Continuing education can help you develop new interests and passions, and expand your worldview.

To make the most of continuing education opportunities, it's important to be intentional about your goals and choose programs or courses that align with your interests and career aspirations. Consider talking to your employer about funding or supporting your continuing education, or seek out scholarships or grants to help finance your studies. In addition to the benefits listed above, continuing education can also lead to increased job security and greater earning potential. By demonstrating a commitment to ongoing learning and professional development, you may be viewed as a valuable asset to your organization or industry. This can lead to opportunities for increased responsibility, higher salaries, and greater job satisfaction.

Another advantage of continuing education is the opportunity to network with other professionals in your field. Attending conferences or workshops can provide valuable opportunities to connect with others who share your interests and goals, and can lead to new collaborations or job opportunities.

While pursuing continuing education can be rewarding, it can also be challenging to balance with other commitments such as work and family responsibilities. It's important to have a clear plan in place and to manage your time effectively to make the most of your education opportunities. This may involve setting specific goals and timelines for completion, breaking down coursework into manageable chunks, and seeking out support from others when needed.

Overall, continuing education is an important investment in

your career and personal growth. By staying up-to-date on the latest trends and technologies in your industry, you can position yourself as a valuable asset to your organization and build a fulfilling and rewarding career.

# MASTERING TIME MANAGEMENT: STRATEGIES FOR BOOSTING PRODUCTIVITY AND ACHIEVING YOUR GOALS

Time management is a skill that can be developed with practice and consistency. One of the keys to effective time management is prioritization. Make a list of your most important tasks each day and prioritize them in order of importance. This will help you to focus your efforts on what matters most and ensure that you are making progress on your most critical projects.

Breaking tasks into smaller, more manageable pieces can also be an effective strategy for improving time management. When faced with a large task, it's easy to feel overwhelmed and procrastinate. However, by breaking the task down into smaller steps, you can make progress more quickly and maintain momentum. This can also help to reduce stress and make the task feel less daunting.

Another important strategy for effective time management is to eliminate distractions. Turn off your phone, close unnecessary browser tabs, and limit interruptions to stay focused and productive. When you are in the middle of an important task, interruptions can be particularly disruptive, causing you to lose focus and momentum. By minimizing distractions, you can maintain your focus and productivity.

Finally, it's important to schedule time for self-care. Taking care of yourself is critical for maintaining productivity and avoiding burnout, so make sure to schedule time for exercise, relaxation, and other self-care activities. This can help to reduce stress and increase your energy levels, making it easier to stay focused and productive throughout the day.

Effective time management is a critical skill for success in any career. By prioritizing your tasks, breaking tasks into smaller pieces, eliminating distractions, and scheduling time for self-care, you can boost your productivity, achieve your goals, and maintain a healthy work-life balance.

# THE FUTURE OF WORK AND INDUSTRIES

As technology continues to evolve at an unprecedented pace, the future of work and industries is becoming increasingly complex. In this section, we will explore some of the key trends and predictions for the future of work and the M&A industry, and examine how these developments will impact businesses and individuals.

# THE FUTURE OF WORK: HOW TECHNOLOGY IS CHANGING THE LANDSCAPE OF YOUR INDUSTRY

Technology has been a driving force behind the transformation of work, and its impact is set to continue. Here are some of the key trends and predictions for the future of work:

Remote work has been growing in popularity for several years, but the COVID-19 pandemic has accelerated the trend. With many companies forced to quickly shift to remote work to comply with social distancing guidelines, the benefits of remote work have become even more apparent.

One of the key advantages of remote work is cost savings. By eliminating the need for office space and reducing overhead costs, companies can save a significant amount of money. Additionally, remote work allows companies to tap into a wider talent pool, without being limited by geography. This can lead to more diverse and skilled teams, and ultimately, better business outcomes.

Remote work has also been shown to increase productivity, as employees are often more focused and able to better manage their time. Furthermore, remote work allows for greater flexibility in scheduling, which can improve work-life balance and reduce employee burnout.

However, remote work also poses some challenges, such as potential isolation and difficulty in maintaining company culture and collaboration. As such, companies will need to implement strategies and technologies to overcome these challenges and support a hybrid model of remote and in-person work.

Overall, the trend towards remote work is likely to continue, and companies that are able to adapt and leverage the benefits of remote work will have a competitive advantage in the future.

The rise of automation has been a major driver of change in the job market, with many routine tasks and jobs being automated through the use of artificial intelligence (AI) and robotics. While this has led to increased efficiency and productivity in many industries, it has also raised concerns about the displacement of workers and the need for reskilling and upskilling.

According to a 2019 report by the McKinsey Global Institute, up to 375 million workers worldwide may need to switch occupations or learn new skills by 2030 as a result of automation and other technological advances. This will require significant investments in education and training programs to ensure that workers have the skills they need to succeed in the jobs of the future.

On the positive side, automation also creates new job opportunities in areas such as data analysis, software development, and cybersecurity. As such, workers who are able to adapt and acquire new skills will be well-positioned to take advantage of these emerging opportunities.

Overall, the rise of automation is set to continue, and workers and companies alike will need to be prepared to navigate the changing landscape of work and industry.

In the past, learning was often viewed as a one-time event that occurred in the first few years of a person's career. However, as the pace of technological change continues to accelerate and jobs become more complex, the need for continuous learning and upskilling has become increasingly apparent.

To stay competitive in the workforce, individuals must continuously learn and adapt to new technology and trends. Companies must also invest in the ongoing education and training of their employees to remain at the forefront of their industries.

Lifelong learning can take many forms, from traditional classroom education to online courses, certifications, and informal learning opportunities such as mentoring or job shadowing. By staying up-to-date on the latest trends and technologies, individuals and companies can better position themselves for success in the future of work.

In addition to benefiting individuals and companies, lifelong learning can also have positive impacts on society as a whole. A more educated and skilled workforce can lead to increased innovation, productivity, and economic growth. Furthermore, ongoing education and training can help individuals develop a greater sense of purpose and fulfillment in their careers, leading to a more engaged and satisfied workforce.

# THE EVOLUTION OF M&A: TRENDS AND PREDICTIONS FOR THE FUTURE OF THE INDUSTRY

As the business landscape continues to evolve, the M&A industry is not immune to change. The trends and predictions that are emerging are poised to shape the industry in the coming years. One such trend is cross-border M&A, where companies look beyond their national borders to expand their reach and access new markets. This trend is particularly important in a globalized world where companies are constantly seeking new growth opportunities.

Another trend that is gaining momentum is digital M&A. Digital M&A refers to the acquisition of technology-focused companies or the purchase of technology-driven assets, such as software platforms, customer data, or proprietary algorithms. The aim of digital M&A is to gain a competitive advantage and enhance a company's digital capabilities, which are essential for businesses to succeed in today's rapidly changing landscape.

One of the driving factors behind the growth of digital M&A is the increasing demand for technology-driven products and services. As more consumers turn to digital platforms to shop, socialize, and work, companies are looking to acquire the technology and assets needed to meet these evolving needs.

In addition, digital M&A can help businesses to gain access to new markets and customer segments. By acquiring a digital company that has a strong presence in a particular market or demographic, businesses can expand their reach and grow their customer base.

Digital M&A can also provide companies with the opportunity to diversify their revenue streams. By acquiring a technology-driven company that has a complementary product or service offering, businesses can expand their offerings and create new revenue streams.

However, digital M&A also comes with its own set of challenges. Integrating digital assets and technologies into existing systems can be complex and time-consuming, and it requires a deep understanding of both the target company's technology and the acquirer's existing systems.

Overall, as technology continues to play an increasingly important role in the business landscape, digital M&A is likely to become an even more important strategy for companies looking to stay competitive and grow their businesses.

Environmental, Social, and Governance (ESG) considerations are increasingly playing a role in the M&A industry. As consumers and investors become more socially conscious and prioritize sustainability, companies are recognizing the need to incorporate ESG considerations into their M&A decision-making process. This can involve evaluating the environmental impact of potential acquisitions, assessing a target company's labor practices, and considering community engagement efforts, among other factors. Additionally, companies are recognizing the long-term benefits of integrating ESG considerations into their business operations and corporate strategy, not just in the context of M&A. As a result, ESG is likely to continue to play a growing role in the

M&A industry and beyond.

Private equity (PE) and venture capital (VC) continue to play a significant role in driving M&A activity. According to a report by PitchBook, global M&A deals involving PE and VC investors reached a record high of $530 billion in the first half of 2021. This indicates that PE and VC firms are highly active and are continuing to seek out opportunities to invest in M&A deals.

In fact, the report also found that there has been a notable shift in the M&A landscape with a growing number of PE and VC firms looking to acquire software and tech-enabled companies. These firms have been attracted to the recurring revenue models and high growth rates of such companies. The technology sector has been especially attractive to PE and VC investors, accounting for a significant portion of the M&A deals in recent years.

As the competition in this space remains fierce, investors are striving to secure the best deals and achieve the greatest returns. The PitchBook report also highlights that there has been an increase in deal sizes, with the average deal size for PE-backed deals rising to $1.5 billion in the first half of 2021. This trend is expected to continue as PE and VC firms look for larger and more strategic deals that can generate substantial returns for their investors.

Overall, the data suggests that PE and VC firms will continue to be a driving force in the M&A industry, with the competition for deals likely to remain intense. As such, companies looking to engage in M&A transactions will need to be prepared to navigate a highly competitive landscape and be well-positioned to secure the best deals.

In today's rapidly evolving business environment, it is more important than ever for companies to be proactive and informed about the latest trends and developments in the M&A industry. This requires a deep understanding of the market conditions and factors that impact M&A activity, as well as a keen awareness of emerging trends and news. By staying up-to-date with these developments, companies can position themselves to be agile and responsive, able to seize opportunities and navigate challenges as they arise. In doing so, they can not only stay competitive but also thrive in the dynamic and constantly evolving M&A landscape.

# CONCLUSION

The landscape of work and industries is rapidly changing, driven by technological advancements, evolving consumer preferences, and shifting market conditions. In this book, we have explored some of the key trends and predictions for the future of work and the M&A industry, from the rise of remote work and automation to the increasing importance of lifelong learning and ESG considerations in M&A decision-making.

We have also examined the role of private equity and venture capital in driving M&A activity, and the need for companies to stay informed and adaptable to succeed in this dynamic and competitive landscape. Through a combination of case studies, data analysis, and expert insights, we have provided a comprehensive overview of the current state and future directions of the world of work and M&A.

As we look to the future, it is clear that the pace of change will only continue to accelerate, and the ability to learn, adapt, and innovate will become even more critical. Our final thoughts and advice to readers are to embrace change and stay curious, to invest in ongoing education and training, and to maintain a growth mindset that enables continuous learning and development.

We call on readers to continue their personal and professional development journey, to seek out new opportunities and challenges, and to be open to the possibilities that the future holds. By doing so, individuals and companies alike can position themselves to thrive in the ever-evolving landscape of work and industries. In the coming years, remote work is likely to become even more prevalent, as companies increasingly recognize the benefits of flexible work arrangements. This will require organizations to continue to invest in technology and digital infrastructure, as well as develop strategies to support and engage remote workers.

Automation is also expected to continue to disrupt jobs and industries, as AI and robotics become even more advanced. This will require individuals and companies to embrace lifelong learning and upskilling, in order to remain competitive and adapt to new roles.

In the M&A industry, we can expect to see continued growth in cross-border M&A and digital M&A, as companies seek to expand their reach and acquire new capabilities. ESG considerations are also likely to play an increasingly important role in M&A decision-making, as sustainability and social responsibility become more important to consumers and investors. Private equity and venture capital are expected to remain strong drivers of M&A activity, as investors continue to seek out new opportunities to grow and diversify their portfolios.

To navigate this rapidly evolving landscape, it is critical for individuals and companies to stay informed and prepared to adapt to new trends and developments. This requires ongoing learning and upskilling, as well as a strong understanding of the market conditions and factors that influence the M&A industry. By staying ahead of the curve and embracing change, individuals and organizations can thrive in the dynamic and exciting future of work and industries.

In conclusion, the future of work and industries is exciting, challenging, and full of opportunity. By embracing change, investing in lifelong learning, and staying informed about emerging trends and developments, individuals and organizations can succeed in this rapidly evolving landscape. We encourage readers to continue their personal and professional development journeys and to stay engaged with the latest news and developments in their respective fields. With hard work, dedication, and a willingness to adapt, the future is bright and full of possibilities.